Pembroke Dock
reflections

by John Evans

Published by
Paterchurch Publications
6 Laws Street, Pembroke Dock, Pembrokeshire SA72 6DL
e-mail: johnevans@paterchurch.freeserve.co.uk
website: www.paterchurch-publications.co.uk

First Printed: November 2001

Design and printed by CIT Brace Harvatt, Haverfordwest

ISBN: 1870745 12 4

All communities can claim to be unique and the town of Pembroke Dock can justify that claim on several counts.

This is a town where some 260 ships were built for the Royal Navy during the 112 years that the Royal Dockyard was active. The town was created from 1814 around that Dockyard. It was here that fine ships were built for Queen Victoria's Navy at a time when Britain ruled the waves and its Empire was expanding across the continents.

To defend the Dockyard soldiers were required and so early on the town began its links with the military. It became a garrison town and many of the famous regiments in the British Army were stationed at one time or another at Pembroke Dock.

The closure of the Dockyard in 1926 was a body blow for the community which many say it has never really recovered from. What was one of the most prosperous towns in Wales became, almost overnight, a community without a purpose and without hope.

The junior service in Britain's military - the Royal Air Force - brought some hope to Pembroke Dock from 1930 when it established a flying-boat station here. What started out as a 'temporary' establishment quickly became permanent and for over 25 years the sounds of aero engines and the sight of majestic flying-boats on the Haven waters and in the air were ever present and comforting. But, like the Dockyard, this had to end and the last Sunderlands departed in 1957. Within a few years the Army had left too.

With all its military establishments - including oil tank farms on either side - Pembroke Dock was a prime target, and in the Second World War it suffered grievously at the hands of the German Luftwaffe. The scars of Pembroke Dock's own 'blitz' still show on the streets of the town.

The postwar years have been turbulent and chequered for this community as it has sought to find a new identity outside of being a military town. It has benefited from the arrival of the oil industry to the Haven, but that has declined considerably over the years, and it has become less isolated thanks to the construction of the Cleddau Bridge which has linked the south of the county with the rest of Pembrokeshire. And, in the past 20 years, there has been a sizeable increase in the population as many new housing estates have been built on the edges of the old Victorian town with its 'gridiron' pattern of wide, elegant streets.

A number of books have been written about Pembroke Dock and its remarkable history. These have included books drawing upon the extensive archives of picture postcards produced by Victorian and Edwardian photographers. It is thanks to these photographers that we have such a fine record of how Pembroke Dock looked a century and more ago.

This particular book sets out to reflect upon the changing face of a Dockyard town in the 20th Century. It starts around the turn of the century when Pembroke Dockyard was at its zenith, and spans the years up to 2000. Much has changed in 100 turbulent years.

PEMBROKE DOCK MUSEUM

A donation from the sale of each book will be made to the Pembroke Dock Museum Trust which this year (2001) took over the running of the Gun Tower Museum in Front Street.

A number of photographs already donated to the Museum Trust are used in this volume. With its own Museum, and exciting plans for the future, the Trust is now in a position to appeal for items, artifacts and photographs relating to Pembroke Dock.

Photographs - on loan - are also sought for a Volume II in this series and contact can be made with the Author at the Paterchurch Publications address.

ACKNOWLEDGEMENTS

I am indebted to several friends who have contributed photographs and allowed open access to their collections. In particular I acknowledge the special help of Keith Johnson and Roger Thomas who have loaned many of the postcards used here. My thanks also go to my journalist colleague and naval specialist Ted Goddard not only for photographs but for detailed information on various vessels, and to another journalist friend, Vernon Scott, for his encouragement and support. The Pembroke Dock Museum Trust members have given me excellent support and Ron Watts, in particular, has been a great help. Trust Chairman Martin Cavaney has also allowed me to use a number of his photographs and I am also grateful to Mr David Evans of the Western Telegraph and to Mr Jon Evans of Studio Jon for permission to use other illustrations. I acknowledge the help of Mr Nic Wheeler, Chief Executive of the Pembrokeshire Coast National Park Authority, who granted permission to use the fine aerial view used as the cover shot, and other individuals who have contributed, along with the Carsley and Lawswood Collections.

Once again the staff of CIT Brace Harvatt have come up trumps completing the production of this book to a very tight and demanding schedule.

Finally, but by no means least, my thanks go to Christine, Rob, Tom and Jonathan for their encouragement and for giving me the incentive and the time to complete this latest book project. Special thanks to Mrs E and Mrs C, my best supporters.

John Evans
Pembroke Dock.
November 2001.

Also by the Author.
Flying-Boat Haven (RAF Pembroke Dock pictorial)
The Sunderland, Flying-Boat Queen Volume I, pictorial
The Sunderland, Flying-Boat Queen Volume II, pictorial
Sopwiths to Sunderlands (History of 210 Squadron, RAF)
Help From The Heavens (History of 228 Squadron, RAF)

Wooden wallers... *Fine ships built for Queen Victoria's Navy was the proud claim of Pembroke Dockyard for much of the 19th Century. This artist's impression captures a stormy day off Pembroke Dock. The sheds over the Dockyard slipways and the Front Street Gun Tower also feature, while two 'wooden wallers' lie at anchor, one with sails unfurling.*
Author's Collection.

Prosperity… *For over a century Pembroke Dock was one of the most prosperous towns in Wales, thanks to its Royal Dockyard. The wage packets earned by the dockyard workers supported families, tradespeople and the many pubs which flourished. All this was to change dramatically when the dockyard closed in 1926. This postcard, showing dockyard workers leaving through the famous gates, is dated 1906. Keith Johnson Collection.*

The Avenue & Dockyard, Pembroke.

Waterfront... *Sheds over the dockyard slipways dominated the waterfront at the turn of the 20th Century when Pembroke Dockyard was at its zenith. This view - postdated 1910 - shows the open land to the south of the dockyard gates. In later years the RAF built houses on these field for their officers and men and named them after flying-boats - Southampton Row, Sunderland Avenue and Catalina Avenue. Author's Collection.*

Panorama...
Fourteen years separate the postmarks on these postcards from the 'Dainty' company, but the shots were taken on the same day, as the children in the foreground testify. Workers are leaving the dockyard and moving up Cumby Terrace - named after a famous Navy Admiral who served at Pembroke Dockyard - into Victoria Road with its fine houses. In the distance, at Hobbs Point, a three funnelled cruiser is 'fitting out'. Author's Collection.

VIEW FROM BARRACK HILL, PEMBROKE DOCK.

PEMBROKE DOCK, FROM BARRACK HILL

Elegance... *The wide streets of Pembroke Dock have an elegance and style. London Road, linking the town to the capital, had two hotels facing each other. On the left in this S. J. Allen postcard is the Pier Hotel with its prominent balcony. Opposite was the Criterion Hotel. Both were destroyed by the Luftwaffe during a night bombing raid on 11th/12th May, 1941. Author's Collection.*

Flying the flag... *A flag flies from the top window of the house on the right in Commercial Row as local children study the cameraman. Commercial Row, just outside the dockyard wall, was the town's business centre for generations. Dockyarders earned their money inside the walls and spent it in Commercial Row. The trees on the left have since grown into mature specimens. Keith Johnson Collection.*

The law... *Two policemen pause for a chat in an uncluttered Bush Street. The Charlton pub is on the right with a building society sign on the house opposite, at the bottom of Upper Park Street. In the early part of the 20th Century cars had yet to intrude onto the streets of the town. This is another S. J. Allen postcard dating from c1908. Keith Johnson Collection.*

***Learning...**
Edwardian
youngsters pose
coyly for the S. J.
Allen photographer
who is focusing on
the newly opened
Coronation Council
School in Upper
Meyrick Street. The
school, built on the
site of the British
School, was opened
on 4th May, 1904.
A century on it is
still a place of
learning as an
adult education
centre.
Lawswood
Collection.*

Railway... *Steam power and horse power still ruled when this photograph of Pembroke Dock's Great Western Railway goods yard was taken c1906. Note the Venus Soap sign on the side of the shed. The railway reached the town in 1864 and Pembroke Dock is still, today, literally at the 'end of the line'. Lawswood Collection.*

Naval power... Some 260 ships were built at Pembroke Dockyard and by the early part of the 20th Century the yard was specialising in the construction of fast cruisers. HMS Duke of Edinburgh, seen here in all her glory, was an armoured cruiser of 13,550 tons launched in 1904. She and her Pembroke Dock-built sisters, HMS Defence and HMS Warrior, were part of the First Cruiser Squadron at the Battle of Jutland in 1916 and only the Duke of Edinburgh survived, the other two being sunk in this action. Duke of Edinburgh was broken up in 1920. Pembroke Dock Museum Trust Collection.

Launching... *An unusual view shortly before the launching on 14th May, 1908, of the 3,300 ton scout cruiser HMS Boadicea. The construction of the covering shed is shown to good effect. Boadicea survived the Great War and was broken up in 1926.*
Keith Johnson Collection.

Fitting out... .A three funnelled 'County Class' cruiser lies alongside Hobbs Point, the fitting out wharf for the dockyard. After being launched from the slipways vessels were brought over to Hobbs Point and fitted out with engines, guns and other equipment. This shot, taken from the hutted encampment at Llanion, dates from the very early years of the last century. Hobbs Point itself dates back to 1832. Keith Johnson Collection.

Pembroke Dock from Huts.

Pembroke Dockyard from Barrack Hill

Writer... *'The five sheds near the water are shipbuilding sheds for battleships - I can't tell you what they are building now' penned the anonymous card writer in February 1916. In the foreground is Victoria Road with the fine terrace of Dockyard buildings behind. This postcard from the Nutshell Press was no doubt published some years before the Great War. Keith Johnson Collection.*

Fine prospect... *'View from Prospect' is the title of this S. J. Allen postcard. This path leading up from Church Street is still in use today. Above it houses look out from Prospect Place over the rooftop view which these youngsters were enjoying in the early days of the century. Keith Johnson Collection.*

Queen Street and Dimond Street, Pembroke Dock

Bush Street, Pembroke Dock

Gridiron... *Pembroke Dock's wide streets set on a gridiron pattern make for fine photographs. Judging by the consecutive serial numbers on these postcards from the Valentine's company the photographs were taken around the same time - or even on the same day. A couple of carts and horses wend their way along Queen Street and Dimond Street (left) while Bush Street is equally quiet. The Star Stores in Bush Street's western end have an impressive awning. This end of Bush Street was to suffer badly in a German air raid in November 1940.*
Author's Collection.

On guard...
Cannons guard the ramparts of the Defensible Barracks - which for over 150 years has commanded a strategic position overlooking the town - in this Harvey Barton postcard dated 1911. Built in 1844-45 on high ground to the south the superbly constructed stone barracks were completed inside a year. Roger Thomas Collection.

The Barracks, Pembroke Dock.

Llanion Barracks, Pembroke Dock

Barracks... *Llanion Hill, to the north of the town, had a military encampment dating from the Crimean War of the 1850s. By 1906 the huts had been replaced by brick-built barracks as seen in this Valentine's card postdated September, 1909. The Colonel's residence and the Officers' Mess are on the left.*
Author's Collection.

Quarters... *The postcard states that these are the New Barracks, Pembroke Dock (quarters of the 2nd Wiltshire Regiment). Writing to an Army friend, Private W. Smith, of F Company of the Wiltshire's, reported his safe arrival to new surroundings.*
Keith Johnson Collection.

Airship... The earliest known aerial view of Pembroke Dock was taken from a Royal Naval Air Service airship stationed at Sageston, Carew, five miles to the east. The Royal Navy established an airship station - known as RNAS Pembroke - there in 1915, its airships operating on maritime patrols. This view shows London Road and, in the centre, the long demolished houses in King William Street. The large gasholder alongside the houses earned the street the nickname 'Gasworks Lane'. To the rear of the London Road houses is the railway spur line which led to Hobbs Point. The main rail line is at the top of the picture. S. E. Taylor Collection via Brian Turpin.

.MEMORIAL PARK. PEMBROKE DOCK.

Memorial... *Servicemen who lost their lives in the Great War are collectively remembered through Pembroke Dock's Memorial Park which was opened in May, 1925. This early view shows a tennis tournament in progress, watched by a crowd. In the distance is the County School, on the corner of Argyle Street and Bush Street, which was completed in 1899. It became the Intermediate School and later the Grammar School before being partly demolished to make way for a new junior school in the 1970s. Keith Johnson Collection.*

'From the Air'...
Just to emphasise the angle the postcard states 'Pembroke Dock from the Air'. Taken by an aerial photography company based at Hendon in London, this view shows how rapidly the town had developed in the century after its founding. The postcard is dated December, 1924. Author's Collection.

PEMBROKE DOCK *from the Ai*

5257

PEMBROKE DOCK.

High and dry... End of the seafaring road
for these vessels was a shoreline 'berth' on
the eastern side of the Dockyard. Probably
dating from the 1920s, this S. J. Allen
postcard was acquired by an RAF airmen
who came to Pembroke Dock around 1932.
Squadron Leader Ron Williams.

End of era... *Local photographer S. J. Allen
took this unusual view over the now
redundant Royal Dockyard following its
closure in 1926. The slipways and the sheds
where so many ships had been constructed
in 112 active years were unused and
unwanted. Truly, an era had ended.
Keith Johnson Collection.*

PEMBROKE DOC

Interior St. John's Church, Pembroke Dock.

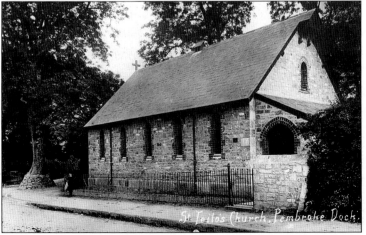

Parish... Featured among Pembroke Dock's fine streets are many places of worship, imposing buildings in their own right. There is a timelessness about the interior of the parish church of St John's, on Bush Street (far left) which dates from 1848. Little has changed in 100 years although the ornate gas lamps have long gone. Two other churches are part of the parish - St Patrick's on Treowen Road, Pennar (top left) and St Teilo's on London Road (left).
Roger Thomas Collection and Author's Collection

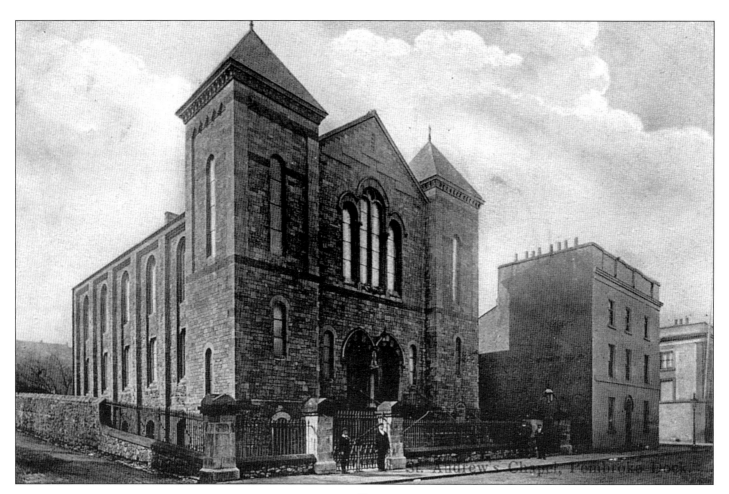

St. Andrew's Chapel, Pembroke Dock

Bethany Baptist Chapel & School,
Pembroke Dock.

Non-Conformity... *The town boasts fine non-Conformist chapels to espouse the Christian cause. St Andrew's Presbyterian Chapel, in Bush Street (far left) has a towered facade alongside the colonial style of Kensington House on the junction of Laws Street.*

Bethany Chapel, in Pennar (top left), is one of three Baptist churches serving the community. Bethany dates from 1877 and had a fascinating 'launch'. It foundation stone was laid in June, 1877, by the Japanese Envoy who was in Pembroke Dock for the launching of an armoured corvette, the Hi Yei, for the Japanese Navy. This was not constructed in the Dockyard but at a private shipyard at Jacob's Pill, Pennar.

The date 1848 is proudly displayed on the front of the very large Wesley Church, in Meyrick Street (bottom left). In recent years it has been renamed Zion Church.

Keith Johnson Collection and Author's Collection.

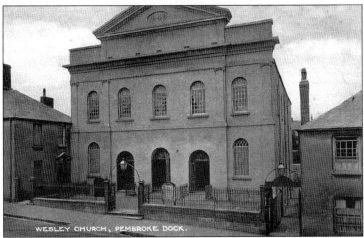

WESLEY CHURCH, PEMBROKE DOCK.

New chapter...

After years of despair and no hope for a forgotten community, Pembroke Dock's fortunes began ever so slowly to upturn as the 1930s dawned. The Royal Air Force, seeking a station for another flying-boat squadron, looked to the Haven Waterway and the former Royal Dockyard. The first squadron - No 210 - flew here in June, 1931. Two of its Southamptons lie at moorings off the slipways, one of which still has its sheds in place. Chris Ashworth Collection.

Engineers... *An early task for the RAF flying-boat personnel was to take aerial photographs of local landmarks. One of these was the Royal Engineers Barracks at Pennar on the prominent headland overlooking the Pembroke River. Pennar Barracks was completed just before the turn of the century and this photograph is dated September, 1932. Its military role ended in the late 1950s and in later years the area became Pennar Park, a holiday site and caravan park reached, appropriately, along Military Road. Mrs L. James.*

New boats... *On waters where naval vessels once launched, RAF Southampton flying-boats ride at their moorings in this S. J. Allen postcard dating from 1934.*
The view over the old dockyard is changing with one of the two giant flying-boat hangars, constructed in the mid 1930s, taking shape on the skyline.
Before the hangars and a slipway suitable for flying-boats were built all maintenance on the aircraft had to be carried out at their moorings, or on board the RAF's unique Floating Dock. Designed by a Pembroke Dock man, Mr John H. Narbeth, the Floating Dock (far right) was in use locally from 1932 until the end of 1938. Nicknamed 'HMS Flat Iron' because of its unglamorous looks, it could accommodate two flying-boats as depicted here with two Southamptons aboard. John Rowlands Collection and Mrs Joyce Skelton.

Pembroke Dock. S.J.A.

Cross channel... Daily life in Pembroke Dock for much of the century included the sights and sounds of the ferries which plied their regular schedules between Hobbs Point and Neyland. Between the start of the car ferry service in 1923 and the arrival of new ferries in the mid 1950s the Alumchine and the Lady Magdalen were the maids of all work. Alumchine, built at Queensferry, North Wales, in 1923, was a coal-fired steam paddler while the Lady Magdelen had a conventional twin-screw configuration. Both soldiered on until 1956 and efforts were made to try and preserve the Alumchine, but these ended in failure and she was scrapped in 1962. Her veteran sister was sold for passenger use on the River Clyde.
The Alumchine is seen (right) approaching Hobbs Point while the Lady Magdelen is pictured (far right) in mid Haven with a full complement of cars and passengers.
Edgar Morgan and Ivor Evans.

Approach... *An S. J. Allen postcard captures the Alumchine on her approach to Hobbs Point. Taken some time before the postdate of November, 1939, the card also shows the Floating Dock and, on the far left, the sheer legs which still towered above the Carr Jetty. The considerable size of the Hobbs Point slipway, used in dockyard days as a fitting out wharf, can be judged from this view.*
Roger Thomas Collection.

PEMBROKE DOCK.

Copyright.
P.D. 4

EAST, PEMBROKE DOCK.

Raphael Tuck & Sons, Ltd
London.

Rooftops... *A favoured view for postcard photographers is from the Barrack Hill. This Raphael Tuck card probably dates from the mid 1930s. The distinctive roof of the Market (centre) and the Co-op building and the Tabernacle Chapel in Albion Square (to the right) stand out. The Luftwaffe's bombs on the town in 1940 and 1941 would change this rooftop view.*
Author's Collection.

DIMOND STREET, PEMBROKE DOCK.

Copyright.
.D. 10

Raphael Tuck & Sons, L
London.

Town centre...
Sun blinds are out on shops in Dimond Street in this pre-war Raphael Tuck postcard. W. H. Smith was for so long a feature on the corner and outside the shop a sign points to the Post Office then located near the Catholic Church in Meyrick Street. Today Barclays Bank still dominates the contemporary view of this street. Author's Collection.

Farewell... Although not dated or marked the 'new-style' RAF uniforms offer a major clue as to when this postcard picture of a service funeral was taken. It is most likely to be December 1938 when RAF Pembroke Dock said farewell to the CO of No 210 Squadron, Wing Commander William Noble Plenderleith, who tragically collapsed and died at the age of just 39. He was buried with full military honours in Llanion Cemetery. The procession is passing along the western end of Bush Street - an area soon to be 'blitzed' in German air raids. Newspaper billboards and a Players Please sign stand outside the newsagents shop. Author's Collection

N959

THE FERRY, PEMBROKE DOCK

Hangar... *Another perspective on the town with the Dockyard Chapel, tucked among the trees, as the centrepoint. The card's title - The Ferry - refers to the ferry Alumchine in the distance. The eastern RAF hangar appears to have been completed yet is only half its final size. A change of plan obviously resulted as the eastern hangar became 'full size' before long.*
Roger Thomas Collection.

Silver ladies... *Five silver Sunderlands ride at moorings off the RAF station in 1939 - the photographer could have waited for the tide to come in! The arrow points to a tiny Walrus single-engined amphibian which was also stationed locally before the war. The writer of the postcard refers to '... ..most of them are now camouflaged.' War clouds were looming large over central Europe and Pembroke Dock was gearing up for action in another conflict.*
Deric Brock Collection.

Old and new... *A remarkable shot, taken by Squibbs Photographers which had offices in Tenby and Pembroke Dock. It can be dated by identifying the aircraft at their moorings. They are Short Singapores of 210 Squadron and Supermarine Stranraers of 228 Squadron - both biplanes - the three of the very new Sunderlands with which both squadrons were to re-equip. The photograph was taken over the roofs of Upper Laws Street and Church Street in the latter part of 1938 before the Floating Dock was towed away from the Haven. St John's Church clock tower is prominent in the centre.*
Roger Thomas Collection.

Making friends... *With the war just a few weeks old Pembroke Dock had its first 'invasion' - from a party of Australian airmen sent over to man a Sunderland squadron. They arrived on Boxing Day, 1939, and among them was a young airman from Victoria, John H. Evans. A lot was made in the press over the Aussies coming to help the Mother Country and John was snapped by a national photographer meeting up with a friendly local! John noted: 'Brass buttons and LAC badge - both had disappeared before long; I was in overalls!' Still resident in Victoria, John has, in recent years, been a regular visitor to Pembroke Dock, retracing some of the steps of his wartime service.*
John H. Evans.

Finest... RAF Pembroke Dock's Officers' Mess, built inside the Dockyard Wall between the Chapel and the line of fine houses known as The Terrace, was reputedly the finest Mess in RAF Coastal Command. This photograph showing its front elevation was taken in 1982 - by the mid 1980s it had been demolished. *Author.*

Gun Tower... Although referred to locally as 'Martello Towers' the two forts which guarded the Royal Dockyard - off Front Street, and in Fort Road - are actually known as Cambridge Gun Towers, dating from the 1850s. The larger of the two, in Front Street, was last used in World War II for anti-aircraft defence. After nearly 50 years it was 'rescued' in the 1990s, completely restored with a new access walkway and opened up as an information centre and museum. The Pembroke Dock Museum Trust has now taken over its running as a town museum. In 1986, when this photograph was taken, a former RAF marine craft tender was moored near the Gun Tower. This has since been taken to Southampton for restoration. *Author.*

Tourism... Pembroke Dock once boasted two tourist attractions - the Sunderland flying-boat and the Motor Museum. Housed in the Dockyard Chapel the Motor Museum was run by Mr and Mrs Chester Smith and had many fascinating exhibits. This photograph is part of a postcard sold at the museum.
Mrs Maureen Connolly.

Imposing... Even when unused and forgotten, the Dockyard Chapel still has an imposing air. This was the view in 1985 - a decade later this fine building had been dreadfully vandalised. It is still salvageable and hopefully a brighter future beckons for this important building in Pembroke Dock's heritage. The new access road to the ferry terminal now runs in front of the Chapel.
Author.

Tanks fire... *A huge column of oily smoke billows over the Admiralty oil tanks at Llanreath after the all too successful German daylight raid on Monday, 19th August, 1940. Three Junkers Ju88 bombers leisurely picked off their target and the resulting blaze was the largest oil fire ever seen in the country. Firemen from many parts of England and Wales fought the fire and five Cardiff firemen lost their lives. Their names are remembered on a memorial at the Pembroke Dock Golf Club now sited where the oil tanks stood. This dramatic shot was taken from the Neyland side of the river. Pembrokeshire Record Office HDX/101/64.*

Blitzed... *The shattered remains of the once proud Pier Hotel and houses in London Road and Tremeyrick Street bear witness to the devastation of the Luftwaffe night raid of 11th/12th May, 1941. The raid, by Heinkel He111 bombers, hit other residential areas as well, including Laws Street, Park View Crescent and the Market district. On a population head count Pembroke Dock was among the heaviest bombed communities in Britain during World War II.*
Roy Hordley.

Digging in... *Soldiers in a trench, some wearing gas masks, take part in an exercise. The location of this early wartime shot - taken by S. J. Allen Photographers - has been identified by military historian Roger Thomas as being Bush Camp, Pembroke Dock.*
Roger Thomas Collection.

Honoured… A sombre scene in Meyrick Street in July, 1942, as the bodies of five Australian airmen are carried out from the Catholic Church during a mass funeral. The young Australians were crewmen of a Wellington bomber which crashed at Milford Haven docks on 19th July. Brought to the nearest RAF station - Pembroke Dock - the airmen were given full military honours as they were laid to rest in the Military Cemetery at Llanion. Their graves remain there to this day. Pembrokeshire Aviation Group archive.

High summer... *By the high summer of 1943 RAF Pembroke Dock was playing a crucial part in the Battle of the Atlantic. With a multitude of tasks its flying-boats ranged far into the Atlantic and the Bay of Biscay, protecting convoys and seeking out the German U-Boats. For several months in 1943 'PD' was home to the United States Navy Squadron VP-63, with their twin-engined Catalina flying-boats. Several 'Cats' are seen alongside Sunderlands in this view. The aeroplanes are easier to spot than the two well camouflaged hangars. RAF Museum P10956.*

Blackout... Wartime blackout curtains drape the doors of the former Dockyard Chapel which during the RAF era had a dual role - as RAF church and Garrison Theatre. This was the centrepoint of the RAF station's social life, staging various reviews and pantomines. The Dockyard Chapel dates from 1831 and is, arguably, Pembroke Dock's second most historic building. Sadly neglected and vandalised in recent years there are now firm indications that it will be returned to former glories. *Miss Janet Phillips Collection.*

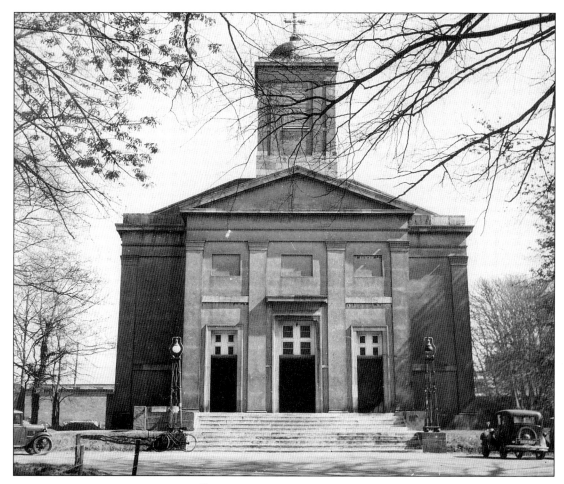

Clock tower... *A prominent dockyard landmark, the clock tower, disappeared after a disastrous fire on 30th November, 1944. Records of No 422 Canadian Squadron state that a minor fire was whipped up by the wind and threatened to destroy the main stores building. The building remains - it now houses the offices for Irish Ferries - but the clock tower was never replaced. Group Captain Guy Bolland.*

Operational... *Sunderlands and the paraphernalia of war lie scattered over the RAF station, including spare floats stored between two of the beautifully constructed former dockyard storesheds. This was RAF Pembroke Dock at its busiest, in mid June 1943. Station Commander Group Captain Alban Carey remembered 99 flying-boats in or around PD at this time - making Pembroke Dock the world's largest operational flying-boat station. Miss Janet Phillips Collection.*

On parade... *The European war just over, the Canadian airmen of No 422 Squadron, RCAF, celebrated their third anniversary in some style at Pembroke Dock, their last wartime station. The formal part of the day - 24th May, 1945 - included a large parade from Llanion Barracks to the RAF Station. Here the RAF station's newly formed pipe and bugle band leads the first of several flights of airmen over the disused railway spur line to Hobbs Point. Military store buildings can be seen on the left. The building in the centre of the photograph is a pump house, later used as a meeting room for the Plymouth Brethren and later still by a fishing club. This pleasing building still stands, now isolated on the Water Street/London Road roundabout. Group Captain Guy Bolland.*

Calm waters... Swans swim serenely in calm waters off Fort Road beach. The war has ended but relics of the conflict remain. Tucked behind the wall in the distance is the RAF bomb stores and the Gun Tower is almost hidden by a 'four-stacker' destroyer which has been beached there. Nearby Pennar Gut mudflats were the final resting place for many redundant naval vessels. With pennant number H82 this was one of some 50 former US Navy vessels given to Britain in 1940. Named HMS Burnham it remained an unusual feature at Fort Road for some time before being scrapped.
Mrs Doris McKay.

Below: A closer view of the old destroyer, the former USS Aulick.
Keith Jobson.

Spoils of war... Days after the war ended in May, 1945, a captured German U-Boat was brought into Pembroke Dock. When taken over by the Royal Navy it had been carrying a cargo of iodine, wolfram and rubber from the Far East and this was removed here. For a short period U-861 was open to the public before being taken to Northern Ireland where it was eventually scuttled. This newspaper report records the U-Boat's arrival.
Author's Collection.

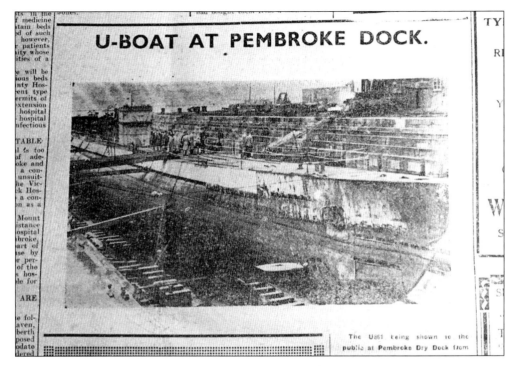

U-BOAT AT PEMBROKE DOCK.

The U861 being shown to the public at Pembroke Dry Dock from

E-Boats... *Old dockyard slipways were also used in the immediate post-war period to store E-Boats - the fast motor torpedo boats used with such good effect by the Germans. Their eventual fate is unknown.*
Danny Kaye.

Hyphen... *An early 1950s view taken at the London Road outskirts of the town. The town name is rather grandly spelt with a hyphen and there is a pedestrian crossing alongside St Teilo's Church. Vic Benson.*

Name... A name long synonymous with Pembroke Dock is motor dealers and bus and coach company W. L. Silcox and Son. Their premises at Waterloo, seen here in the early 1950s, have long since been transformed into a modern car showrooms and filling station. Vic Benson.

Grazing... Cattle graze on the slopes of the Barrack Hill in another familiar view, this time probably dating from the 1950s. The RAF's eastern hangar is now a prominent marker on the skyline. Keith Johnson Collection.

Umbrellas up... On a wet November Sunday the people of Pembroke Dock remember their war dead at the Armistice Service and parade in Bush Street. Soldiers from Llanion Barracks lead the standards and the parade of ex-servicemen. Undated, this photograph was probably taken in the late 1940s or early 1950s. Author's Collection.

Royal occasion... *In August, 1955, Queen Elizabeth II paid her first visit to Pembrokeshire, and her stepping off point from the Royal Yacht Britannia was the RAF Station pier. The smiling Queen is pictured with Air Vice-Marshal Geoffrey Tuttle who welcomed her ashore.*
Squadron Leader Alan Nicoll.

Welcome arch... *In a move reminiscent of Dockyard launching days a 'welcome arch' was erected at the top of Prospect Place for the Queen's visit. A similar arch had marked the launching, in 1899, of the Royal Yacht Victoria and Albert.*
Mrs Winnie Best.

Taking over... *By the late 1950s the car was definitely taking over on the streets of Pembroke Dock. This view of Dimond Street shows that Pembroke Dock's daily problem of cars parking on both sides of the street is nothing new! Barclays Bank has had a re-vamp - this building looks very similar over 40 years on. Roger Thomas Collection.*

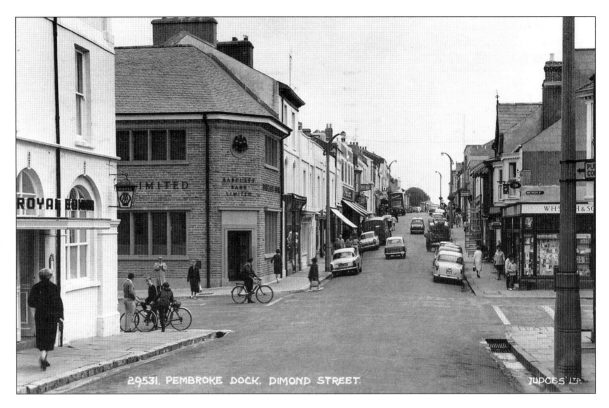

29531. PEMBROKE DOCK. DIMOND STREET.

JUDGES LTD

Conversion... *Resplendent in her new name, new colours and new-look bow, the cable ship Ocean Layer lies off Pembroke Dock following her launching in July, 1955. The 4,800 ton vessel was converted from a former German-built cargo ship, the Empire Frome, by local shipbuilding company R. S. Hayes Ltd and the transformation - done in very quick time - represented a considerable achievement for the firm. The Ocean Layer's maiden voyage was to the Skagerrak to lay the 67-mile telephone cable between Norway and Denmark.*
R. S. Hayes Maritime Collection/Pembroke Dock Museum Trust.

Down the slip... The last major vessel to be built at Pembroke Dock was the trawler Norrard Star which went down the slip at R. S. Hayes' on 10th July, 1956. For the next 30 years the Norrard Star's home port was Milford Haven and she was a regular sight alongside Milford Fishmarket. In 1992 this trawler, historic in her own part of the world, made an unheralded return to her birthplace, being beached off the Haven Maritime premises in Front Street (right). George Lord/R. S. Hayes Maritime Collection, and the Author.

Frigate... R. S. Hayes Ltd completed another major contract in 1957 when refitting work was undertaken on the Royal Navy frigate HMS Porlock Bay, seen undergoing trials in the Haven. The Bay Class frigate, launched in June 1945, was sold to the Finnish Navy in 1962.
R. S. Hayes Maritime Collection/Pembroke Dock Museum Trust.

Venerable... *A once so familiar sight - a Sunderland undergoing maintenance in the RAF station. By 1957 the Sunderlands were reaching the venerable stage and, with no replacements forthcoming, the end of the flying-boat era - and inevitably RAF Pembroke Dock - was predictable. The two local squadrons disbanded in January 1957 and the last Sunderland flew out in March. The RAF Ensign was finally lowered over the station in 1959, ending a short but very special chapter in the town's history. Flight/Sunderland Trust archive.*

Preservation... *In March, 1961, Pembroke Dock welcomed home an 'old lady' - Sunderland ML824 presented by its last operators, the French Navy, to the newly formed Sunderland Trust. For the next ten years what was referred to as 'The last of the Sunderlands' was on display in PD, from where it had operated at the war's end with 201 Squadron. Unfortunately the Sunderland had to remain on outside display, alongside the Dockyard Chapel, and the weather and salt-laden air took their toll of the airframe. In 1971 the decision was taken to present the Sunderland to the newly established RAF Museum in London and ML824 left in pieces for its new home. Today this wonderful aircraft is on view in all its glory in the Museum's Battle of Britain Hall. What might have been, had PD kept its Sunderland, will always be a matter of conjecture locally. Sunderland Trust archive.*

64

Queen and King... A new generation of ferryboats, designed to cater for the motorcar, plied the Hobbs Point - Neyland beat from the mid 1950s. Named the Cleddau Queen and Cleddau King, both vessels were built for the County Council at Hancocks Shipbuilding Co yard in Front Street, Pembroke Dock. The Queen, built as an oil fired steam paddler, was launched in January, 1956, and was later converted to diesel. The King followed in 1962. She was diesel powered with propellers at both ends for better handling and boasted the luxury of ramp access. With the collapse during construction of the Cleddau Bridge in 1970 the ferries had to soldier on until 1975, the King making its last ever fare-paying trip on 8th March - earning a champagne farewell. The Cleddau Queen was sold for civil engineering work in the North of England while her sister found a new role in Northern Ireland on Strangford Lough. Renamed PortaferryFerry, she was recently retired and put up for sale. Both Ivor Evans.

NEYLAND - HOBBS POINT FERRY   M.V. CLEDDAU KING

All change... *Much has altered in the old dockyard since this close up aerial view was taken of the western side in the late 1960s or early 1970s. Some of the former dockyard storehouses have been demolished and the old RAF airmen's quarters (centre right) are also no more. A large lorry park now dominates the area in the centre of the photograph. Biggest changes though have been the construction of the ferry port for the Irish service and the Port of Pembroke wharf. These modern developments spelt the end for most of the Pembroke Dockyard slipways, each unique in size. Defensible Barracks can be seen on the left skyline together with houses and a water tower in Military Road, and a solitary oil tank on the right. R. S. Hayes Maritime Collection/Pembroke Dock Museum Trust.*

Disaster... A Royal Navy photographer from RNAS Brawdy took this dramatic shot from a helicopter on the afternoon of Tuesday, June 3rd, 1970 - the day disaster struck when the southern section of the new Cleddau Bridge collapsed. A box girder section was being moved into place when the structure fell into a gap between two Pembroke Ferry houses. In those seconds four workmen were killed and others injured. It was another five years before the Cleddau Bridge - linking at long last the two shores of the Haven - was completed.
Author's Collection.

Film set... Not a flashback to the Great War but a scene from a 1974 BBC drama programme which used the Defensible Barracks as a film set. The Barracks complex, then owned by the County Council, lent itself splendidly to the period drama. In the 1980s the Barracks were sold into private ownership.
Don Jones.

Prefab... After World War II the housing shortage was addressed by building temporary homes which went universally by the name of 'Prefabs'. Pembroke Dock was one such community - its prefabs were located on the Britannia Estate, Bufferland. These were home sweet home for a generation of Pembroke Dock families and only made way for new housing in the 1980s. This prefab has the words 'District Nurse' on the gate.
Mrs Winnie Best.

Bird's eye view...
A splendid early 1970s view of the Dockyard with all its slipways, including the RAF flying-boat slip, intact. Of these the Graving Dock on the far left is one of the three survivors. The walkway out into the Haven from alongside the Front Street Gun Tower shows to good effect at low tide.
Studio Jon.

Street scenes… *Emulating the postcard photographers of old, these street scenes reflect the changing face of a Victorian town. On the left is Queen Street, and right is Dimond Street on a wet day, from the Star Corner junction. Both date from the late 1970s.*
Western Telegraph.

To Ireland... *A new and important chapter for Pembrokeshire began in May, 1979, when the B&I Company opened a ferry service between Pembroke Dock and Rosslare. Making the maiden voyage was the 6,000 ton Connacht. Since then several large ferries have serviced the route on a twice-daily schedule and are an everyday sight in the Haven and alongside the Pembroke Dock ferry terminal. This photo of the Connacht was not taken locally. Carsley Collection.*

Shipyard... *The old Hancocks Shipbuilding Yard in Front Street, where the two 'royal' Haven ferries were built, seen after it fell into disuse. It was later used by the Haven Maritime company and now, after another period out of use, is likely to be part of redevelopment proposals for the waterfront. Lawswood Collection.*

Warrior!... *What is perhaps Pembroke Dock's most famous vessel was not even built at the town. For over 50 years the ironclad HMS Warrior, dating from 1860, fulfilled a mundane role as a pontoon for the Admiralty oil tanks at Llanion. Berthed just above Pembroke Ferry this historic hulk was well maintained and this proved to be her salvation. While other battleships had all gone to the scrapyard, Warrior survived into an age when her place in naval history was appreciated and she was preserved. In 1979 the old Warrior was towed from Pembroke Dock to Hartlepool where she was restored to her Victorian finest. Today HMS Warrior is on public view at Portsmouth, close to Nelson's famous flagship, HMS Victory. The photograph was taken from the Cleddau Bridge on 29th August 1979.*
Ted Goddard Collection.

Left: Magnificent Warrior entering Portsmouth after her restoration.
Western Telegraph.

Space age!...
Pembrokeshire entered the space age in 1979 when a 'flying saucer' appeared in one of the giant hangars in the old RAF station. Constructed in secrecy it was not destined for Mars but instead was set for stardom in a sequel to the hit film 'Star Wars'. Pembroke Dock's own spaceship - standing 16 feet high and weighing 16 tons - was made in three months by Marcon Fabrications. Equipped with 'hover pads' it could fly - but only at a height of about one and a half inches! Author's Collection.

Familiar... Some familiar business names still remain in Dimond Street, but others have merged into history. This photograph, on a 1970s Archway postcard, shows the street before the St Govan's Centre - next to Woolworths - was built.
Author' s Collection.

Whiteout!... No-one living in south Pembrokeshire in January, 1982, will ever forget the snow which blanketed the area in a few hours - and cut off Pembroke Dock and the surrounding area for several days. A 'wartime spirit' prevailed among residents as they coped with the worst snows since 1947. The only way around was on foot and conditions were extremely difficult as evidenced by the 'ice rink' pavement in this shot taken in Dimond Street.
Author.

Centre... An 'open' glimpse of Dock Street before the new St Govan's Centre building was built right alongside. The picture is dated October, 1982.
Western Telegraph.

Junction... *The junction of Ferry Lane with London Road is a location which, almost without anyone realising it, has changed in recent years. It has been completely remodelled and a pedestrian walkway has been driven through the railway embankment behind. Pedestrians no longer need to play 'Russian roulette' in the road tunnel every time they walk this way.*
Lawswood Collection.

Pump House... The Water Street - London Road junction is another which has been completed revamped. This view, taken in August, 1983, shows the old Pump House tucked away on the left - it is now in the centre of a roundabout. *Western Telegraph.*

Western Way... Major land reclamation works on Pembroke Dock's waterfront also led to a new road being built, partly along the route of the old railway line to the Dockyard. The road - now known as Western Way - was cut between the gardens of King Street and Front Street, which are seen in the foreground. This superb aerial view was taken in the mid 1980s before the road was begun - it was officially opened in December, 1990. *Western Telegraph.*

Tabernacle... *One of the town's most impressive buildings was the Tabernacle Chapel in Albion Square - also known as the Albion Hall. Dating from 1867 its towering front dominated the square. By the early 1980s, when this photograph was taken, it had fallen into disuse, with windows broken and ivy creeping up the walls. Within a few years it was demolished, eventually being replaced by a block of apartments.*
Author.

History recreated... A Catalina landed off Pembroke Dock in September, 1987 - recalling the days when the flying-boats ruled the Haven waters and the skies above. The Catalina - seen here off Hobbs Point - was star of the show at the Pembroke Dock Flying-Boat Reunion, and made a return visit for the 1990 Reunion. In all five Flying-Boat Reunions were staged between 1985 and 1995, bringing many hundreds of former 'boatmen' back to their ' PD' haunts. Martin Cavaney Photography.

The last one... *In September, 1995, work began to demolish the last of the brick-built former airmen's quarters in the old Dockyard, ending another link with the flying-boat era. The whole area has, in very recent years, been turned into industrial land. Hopefully a new era of prosperity will be built around the historic Dockyard site.*
Author.

Glimpse... *An institution in the town for so many years was Monti's Café in Dimond Street. In 1993 Monti's served its last coffee and closed its doors. As the builders moved in so townspeople were given a rare glimpse of the back of buildings in Meyrick Street. Boots the Chemists now stands on the site. Martin Cavaney Photography.*

Legacy... In October, 1998, work for the Pembrokeshire Housing Association to convert redundant shops at the western end of Bush Street revealed a famous name. In flaking paint on an old shop facade was the name Samuel J. Allen, Photographer and Stationer. It is especially thanks to Samuel J. Allen, the best known of the town's photographers, that so many splendid images of this historic town have survived and are able to appear in books like this one. That is Allen's legacy.
Author.

Through the wall... As the century drew to a close a new road route was made into the former Dockyard by opening up an entrance through the dockyard wall by the Market. This March, 1999, view was taken shortly before the wall was breached.
Author.

Nostalgia... There was a nostalgic - if temporary - return for the Pembroke Dock-Neyland ferry service in the autumn of 1999 when the Westfield Pill road bridge near Neyland was closed for major repairs, so cutting off a vital link to the south of Pembrokeshire. An ex-Royal Navy launch, Penguin, ran a very regular service for foot passengers between Hobbs Point and the Neyland Marina pontoon, reviving memories of the old ferries which were once such a part of the Haven scene.
Author.

Military... The special links between Pembroke Dock and the British Army are recalled in a very tangible way - through a Chieftain tank which was presented by the Army to the town. The tank now 'guards' the Western Way route near the Water Street/London Road roundabout. Between the two wars an early Army tank dating from the Great War was displayed at the Memorial Park before being scrapped.
Author.

Centuries... *Tucked inside the Dockyard wall and now overlooked by the South Pembrokeshire Hospital is the town's most historic building - pre-dating Pembroke Dock by many centuries. This is the Paterchurch Tower, probably part of a fortified manor house which stood, with a few farms, on the site chosen for the naval dockyard which transferred from Milford in 1814. Well restored and maintained, the Paterchurch Tower will, it is hoped, form part of an ' historic trail' around Pembroke Dock linking to the Dockyard, the gun forts and other buildings which have played their part in the story of a unique and still young community.*
Author.